ELECTRIC AVEN

The story of Morrison-Electricar

by Keith Roberts

First published in Great Britain in 2010
by Bryngold Books Ltd.,
Golden Oaks, 100 Brynau Wood, Cimla,
Neath, South Wales SA11 3YQ.

www.bryngoldbooks.com

Typesetting, layout and design
by Bryngold Books

ISBN 978-1-905900-16-9

**Printed in Wales
by Gomer Press
Llandysul, Ceredigion.**

CONTENTS

DEDICATION

**I am delighted to dedicate this book
to my lovely grand daughter Ella.**

ABOUT THE AUTHOR

Keith Roberts was born in Swansea in 1943. His lifetime hobby has been the history and restoration of vintage commercial vehicles. He served a five year electrical apprenticeship with ICI (Metals Division) Ltd. He remained with ICI specialising in the maintenance of overhead cranes and that company's fleet of battery electric industrial trucks. Together these two subjects combined for his future career path. Work with a battery electric vehicle distributor in Birmingham was followed by a post with Austin Crompton Parkinson Electric Vehicles Ltd in Leicester, builders of the Morrison Electricar vehicles which feature in this book. Responsible for the company's marketing activities, he was involved in its transfer in 1968 to a new factory at Tredegar, South Wales. After a few years Keith joined Lansing Bagnall Ltd, then the largest British manufacturer of battery electric materials handling equipment. After 10 years he rejoined his old employer in Tredegar by now renamed Crompton Electricars and remained there until the factory closed in 1982. He ended his involvement with the electric vehicle industry with a components manufacturer and retailer. Keith has previously written a magazine article on the history of Morrison Electricar. This book is a unique opportunity to share his deeper research into what was, at its zenith a ground-breaking and innovative business.

APPRECIATION

I should like to extend my gratitude to members of the Morrison family for sharing details on the early years of this fascinating company. My thanks are also due to friends in Birmingham especially those at the Wythall Museum of Transport and all the others without whose help this book would not have come to fruition.

Innovation and endeavour

In the 21st Century more and more focus is being placed on the development of planet-saving, low carbon, electric vehicles. Many believe this 'plug in and go' mode of travel is a breakthrough in our quest for the transport of the future.

Electrically powered vehicles are nothing new however. They have been around for a considerable time. Once again it was a case of Britain leading the world. One company in particular was at the forefront – Morrison-Electricar. This book tells the story of that business from start to finish, with details of its various products and key events in its chequered history.

It is a fascinating story of endeavour and inspiration, a true tale of advances, innovation and change. This is mainly an account of the road-going vehicles produced for the home market. The company also produced industrial trucks and vehicles for export. Information on these is less readily available though they are touched on as the story unfolds. Two sons of AE Morrison, the company's founder, provided much assistance in gathering details of its early history. Subsequent historical data was provided from archive material and, information on the later years, from the author's personal recollections of working with the company's busy marketing department.

When the touring Australian cricket team played at the Grace Road Ground in Leicester, during May 1934 Morrisons were about to export their first chassis to that country. The company grasped the opportunity for a promotional photo shoot combining chassis and cricket officials. Pictured from left to right are: Messrs A C Morrison, E A Morrison, Harold Bushley from Tasmania, Australia; Lord Hazlerigg, Mr. Grimmett, one of the Australian players and NH Wheeler from Colmore Depot in Leicester who were ME distributors. Photo by kind permission of Mrs M. Allen (formerly Morrison).

DELIVERING A REVOLUTION

Surrounded by a multitude of 21st Century transport innovations few people today, particularly youngsters, would be able to accurately describe a road-going, battery-powered electric commercial vehicle.

Despite this, at one time they were a familiar sight and sound on our roads and part of everyday life. From the 1950s through to the 1970s the most obvious, and numerous must surely have been the vehicles that delivered our daily pinta. Sadly they are now rare, as changes in lifestyle and supermarket competition have signalled the demise of milkmen and many other doorstep delivery people, who relied on battery electric road vehicles. As they vanished, so too did their familiar electric vehicles. Their own part in saving the planet passing almost unnoticed.

Battery electric vehicles not only played a major part in doorstep deliveries, but also fulfilled many other roles. They could often be seen at work in hospitals, engaged in municipal duties such as street cleaning, or working at industrial sites and airports to name just a few. To cater for the demand this created, there were several battery electric vehicle manufacturers. At the peak of their popularity, one stood out. Morrison-Electricar claimed to be the UK's – and possibly the world's – largest battery electric road vehicle (BERV) manufacturer.

The company's route to success began back in the 1890s when Alfred Ernest Morrison set up a small engineering business in Dover Street, Leicester. The exact start-up date is unclear; some early literature refers to an 1890 launch, but other sources suggest 1896. According to his family, Alfred was given £22 by his father to set up a business. He was described as an interesting, patient and clever individual with an inventive engineering mind and regarded by some as a forward thinker.

The first products of his business included bicycles, motorcycles, fore-carriages for tricycles and an independently sprung wheel for motorcycle sidecars. This was patented and sold well. After a few years the company diversified into the manufacture of gas-powered stationary engines used

Morrison equipment inside a cinema projection room.

A motorcycle combination with Morrison sidecar and sprung wheel, about 1914-18.

to drive generating sets for lighting, compressors and water pumps. All these items were designed and produced at the works. To illustrate the company's commitment to quality, all new gas engines were rotated from an external source for several hours to allow the bearings to bed in. Later, the machines were dismantled, components checked, and the machines reassembled.

Many generating sets were supplied to large country houses to provide lighting in conjunction with lead acid batteries. It is recorded that during celebrations for the relief of Mafeking during the Boer War, a generator set was supplied to a Leicester hotel which used it to provide power for a patriotic display of red, white and blue lights. At the beginning of the 20th

Century, the company – then known as AE Morrison & Co – started producing Tiger motorcycles. AE also designed and built a small tri-car using a continental Fafnir or Precision engine with flat belt drive to the rear wheel. According to the family, only one was ever made. During this period, the company moved from Dover Street to Gartree Street. Production of gas engines using petrol and other fuels continued to be the main manufacturing function.

During the First World War the business was involved in repairs to agricultural machinery and undertook specialist work for the Government. AE Morrison himself was employed by the War Office to travel around the country lecturing and advising manufacturers on production techniques. To do this he was given a military rank. Coincidentally, his eldest son – AC Morrison – was to perform a similar role during the early years of the Second World War.

At the end of the First World War AE Morrison & Co restarted the manufacture of stationary engines for generators and compressors. The family believe that cars were also produced although no records have been found to support this. Mass production methods used by other manufacturers meant that Morrison's motorcycles and bicycles became uneconomic and their manufacture ended.

The business continued to grow however and 1921-22 brought a move to larger premises, this time in Grace Road, Leicester. The Gartree Street site was retained as office accommodation. At this time the company began targeting a new market with its range of chargers for automotive batteries. There was also a demand for radio battery recharging.

Around 1927-28, the film industry was becoming excited by experimentation with talking pictures, the sound being stored on disc and later on the film itself. AE Morrison was quick to become involved and was soon manufacturing and installing cinema equipment across the UK and overseas. With their expertise in electrical engineering, a range of equipment was manufactured. Brochures from the era illustrate this. One important design was for an electric motor which could run at a constant speed. Without this the music would be reproduced with the effect of a gramophone in dire need of winding. Running on DC supply the Morrison motor was interesting because it had a nickel frame instead of the usual cast iron one and carried thin armature laminations instead of the customary thicker stampings.

An electrifying idea

In 1929, AE Morrison & Co changed its name to AE Morrison & Sons to reflect the entry into the business of AE's relatives such as eldest son AC Morrison, someone who would go on to play a major role. Indeed, it was he who brought battery electric road vehicles into the portfolio. Like many interesting business opportunities, the idea was born on the golf course. In 1933, when AC was playing a round at Leicester's Birstall golf course

with local baker Mr Squires, he was asked whether he could make a vehicle that could deliver goods quicker and cheaper than the bakery's horse. An electric machine was considered the best option and a prototype, based entirely on Morrison ideas, was produced within a month. It was fitted with an ENV rear axle as used by many other vehicle manufacturers such as the Standard Motor Company of nearby Coventry. This prototype had a home-made truck body and carried the registration number JF 3806. This vehicle remained with the company for many years as a works runabout. It used a method of drive which transferred power to the rear offside wheel only via a worm drive from the motor shaft. This was not used in later production models as trials suggested the need for alterations. These included a strengthening of the chassis members and an increase in the wheelbase. The result of this was a load capacity of 10 or 12cwt. AC didn't want to part with the improved prototype to his golfing buddy Mr Squires. However the baker did take delivery of the first production

Complete with spoked wheels,
this was the prototype ME vehicle. Seen here in
1933, it was used as the works runaround for many years.

A line-up of the 600 model straight off the production line soon after the company had moved to its new Brunswick Street factory at South Wigston, Leicester, in 1935.

vehicle. It was fitted with a coach-built body and in 1933 registered as JF 4231. Other businesses were impressed and orders for the electric vehicles began to pour in. Each carried a large Morrison-Electric badge on the cab front. For a short time, an additional badge was fixed to the front of each vehicle, either above or below the main badge. On the 10 and 12cwt models, this carried the model name Terrier, on the 25cwt model it carried the model name Mastiff. The company were not slow to market their product and in 1934 were sending out colour brochures of their growing product range.

In the same year the Australian cricket team was touring the UK. The legendary Don Bradman, who was later knighted, visited the

Morrison factory accompanied by civic dignitaries. Later, a chassis and a completed vehicle were taken to Leicester's Grace Road cricket ground where several of the Australian party were photographed inspecting the chassis before its despatch for Australia.

Even then, export opportunities were pursued enthusiastically and according to George Morrison around 28 chassis were supplied in CKD (completely knocked down) form to Australia. Bodywork and batteries were supplied locally. Other countries recorded as having Morrison Electricar vehicles included New Zealand and Finland, with left-hand drive options available. Success with electric vehicle products saw the company decide to concentrate on these. The stationary engines,

Work underway on the final batch of Electricar refuse vehicles for Birmingham Corporation's salvage department in 1944.

generators and compressors were phased out of production. How long this process took is not known, but a letterhead dated 13 July 1933, shows a wide range of products still available.

The earliest battery electric road vehicle brochure unearthed is dated November 1933. It describes four new models to be made available the following year. These had carrying capacities of 10, 12, 25 and 30cwt. The brochure shows Morrison's interesting drive train, with its electric motor mounted under the driver's seat, a multiple chain enclosed in a case on the output shaft and a tubular shaft to the rear differential unit. A slogan on the brochure's front cover proclaimed: 'The world's largest production because they are the world's best!' It is worth remembering that at this

point, the company had been making electric vehicles for less than a year! Constantly on the lookout for new products to hit fresh markets, the company introduced a novel design for an electric vehicle in late 1934. It was called the Trilec. This interesting three-wheeler had two steerable wheels at the front and a fixed, chain-driven wheel at the rear. Its appearance was not unlike motorcycle-engined delivery vehicles made by Croft Commercial Cars Ltd and John Warrick & Co. A driver sat on a seat mounted on a cowl over the rear wheel and, when driving forward, would look over the load. Power was provided by a mid-mounted Morrison-Electric motor. This drove the rear wheel through a chain mechanism. The battery was mounted pannier fashion and control came

Portsea Island Mutual Co-operative Society bought a large number of vehicles from Morrison-Electricar including this 10cwt bakery van supplied in late 1935.

via a series-parallel controller. Optimistic about this design Morrison's issued a hand-tinted colour brochure in early 1935 giving details of all the options available. However, despite the offer of canopies and other body options, there was no escaping from the fact that this vehicle offered insufficient weather protection for the driver who also suffered a lack of visibility over his load. Few of these vehicles were ever produced as such factors contributed to the design's commercial failure.

Something that the company did achieve successfully however was the manufacture themselves of many of the components for their vehicles. The chassis was built in one part of the factory, the motor and controller in another. Axles and braking systems were outsourced and because of space limitations at Grace Road, bodies were manufactured in Loughborough by the Brush Electrical company.

In 1935 AE Morrison & Sons were once again on the move, this time relocating to a factory in South Wigston, just south of Leicester. Originally

known as the Brunswick Works, it later became the Morrison Works. Here, they they were able to build complete vehicles so the bodywork came back in-house. Around this time nearly all the Morrison family were involved in the business. AE Morrison was managing director, his sons AC Morrison, GH Morrison and FH Morrison were technical director, works manager and in charge of the service department and customer liaison respectively. AE's daughters, Mary Morrison and May Morrison, ran the offices. May – later Mrs May Allen – was the last surviving family member in the business, retiring in 1965.

By the mid-1930s, the company boasted a wide range of chassis sizes with payloads of 5/8 cwt in the 600 series, 10/12 cwt, 18/22 cwt, 25/30 cwt and two to three tons. Bodies at this time included the open dairy option, the closed van and a streamlined choice known as the Airline and available only on the 600 series and the 10/12cwt models. This was a strange looking vehicle with a deep rearwards-sloping body. Another 600 variant was the Airflow. This had a normal control driving position, similar in appearance to those of petrol-engined vehicles. Flat-deck lorry bodies were available and there were specialist designs for the refuse collection market. Each vehicle dashboard had a clock and each driver was supplied with a lapel badge!

Several patents were taken out in connection with the traction motor and controller. In the early days much time and effort was spent in developing a foot-operated accelerator control unit to phase the battery voltage to the traction motor. If the voltage had been applied in full it would damage the motor and possibly destroy the transmission. The time taken from standing start to full speed was around seven seconds. The delay stages controlled a number of electro-mechanical contactors which in turn controlled the voltage from battery to motor. This was achieved through a grid resistance beneath the vehicle's floor. By now a move to standard series battery/motor control had been made from the original series/parallel arrangement. In the original patented foot switch controller, the delays were effected via an Airvane, a small mechanical unit housed in a metal cylinder at the top of the foot switch. This created delays of one and a half seconds per stage; the driver could put his foot to the floor immediately and delays would still come in controlled sequence. Later foot control units used a pneumatic delay mechanism and these

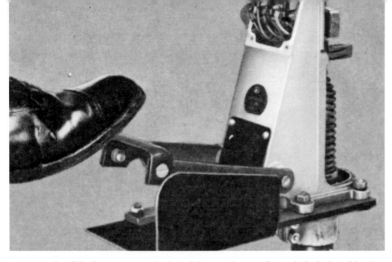

An example of the later pneumatic time delay accelerator footswitch designed by the Morrison-Electricar company.

Workmen engaged in the construction of composite bodied vehicles at the company's Brunswick works during 1936.

continued in use on all vehicles for many years. Experiments were also carried out using a fluid flywheel between the motor and the rear differential, but no production followed due to the cost of such a unit.

Another interesting design was a three-wheeled electric articulated unit built for tests with the Midland Railway Company in 1936. The drive unit was mounted above the front wheel and the whole vehicle looked rather like a back to front Trilec. A standard Scammell coupling was used for the trailer. This vehicle never went into production however, because, while it worked well according to its designer AC Morrison, it couldn't stand up to the heavy workloads of its petrol-engined competitors.

This vehicle featured in the February 28, 1936 issue of Commercial Motor with special interest focussed on the chassis and drive train. A few years later it formed the basis of a successful design as the continuing good relationship between AE Morrison & Sons and Brush Electrical bore fruit. Around 1940 Mr Tom Keene of Brush Electrical Engineering asked AC Morrison to design a small battery electric tractor unit for internal duties. Such a vehicle had not been found on the open market and Brush wished to make one themselves. AC set about the task and scaled-down a version of the three-wheel design used for the Midland Railway Company trials.

Brush set about manufacture, and the truck was so successful that when they had built enough machines for their own use, they made them for others. One large 1941 order from the Ministry of Supply saw a quantity built for shipping to Russia. These industrial trucks were a catalyst for Brush's own battery electric vehicle company which started production of road vehicles in 1945 and eventually became a competitor for Morrisons. Coincidentally, many years later, after Brush had abandoned road vehicle manufacture, their remaining products were absorbed into the Morrison business through a connection with the Hawker Siddeley group. They provided a welcome addition to the Morrison industrial truck range.

Around 1936 AE Morrison & Sons designed a special machine for railway companies to improve the efficiency of moving freight from goods wagons to road vehicles. Based on the company's 25cwt chassis, it was a low-speed mobile platform which could travel forwards or backwards at 2-3mph with an indicator light above a control panel showing which position the direction switch was in. The deck height was the same as that of rail wagons. Fixed platforms and drop plates were lowered to bridge the gap so that barrows and sack trucks could operate between wagons and platforms. A wagon would be unloaded, its goods sorted on the mobile

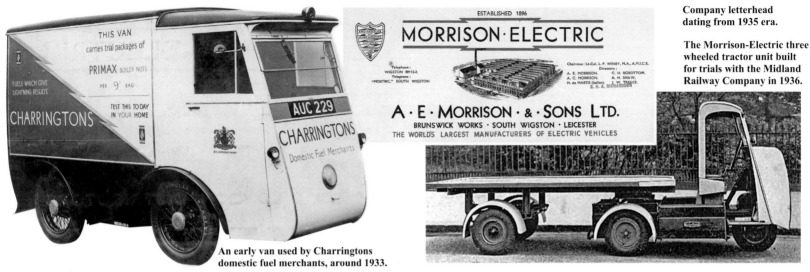

THIS VAN
carries trial packages of
PRIMAX BOILER NUTS
PER 9ᵈ BAG
TEST THIS TO-DAY
IN YOUR HOME

FUELS WHICH GIVE
LIGHTNING RESULTS

CHARRINGTONS

AUC 229

CHARRINGTONS
Domestic Fuel Merchants

BY APPOINTMENT

An early van used by Charringtons domestic fuel merchants, around 1933.

ESTABLISHED 1896

MORRISON·ELECTRIC

Telephone:
WIGSTON 89112-3.
Telegram:
"MORTRIC," SOUTH WIGSTON

Chairman: Lt-Col. L. F. WINBY, M.A., A.M.I.C.E.
Directors:
A. E. MORRISON.   C. H. ROBOTTOM.
A. C. MORRISON.   A. H. SHAW.
H. de MARTIS (Italian).   J. W. TREECE.
E. H. A. RICHARDSON.

A·E·MORRISON·&·SONS LTD.
BRUNSWICK WORKS · SOUTH WIGSTON · LEICESTER
THE WORLD'S LARGEST MANUFACTURERS OF ELECTRIC VEHICLES

Company letterhead dating from 1935 era.

The Morrison-Electric three wheeled tractor unit built for trials with the Midland Railway Company in 1936.

platform, paperwork carried out and the platform would then be driven to waiting road vehicles. This avoided a lot of trans-shipping by previous methods. Incidentally, the travelling platforms were fitted with extended deep-sprung buffers used to move rail wagons by pushing from the rear.

A UNITED APPROACH

In 1936 a new business organisation called Associated Electric Vehicle Manufacturers Ltd (AEVM) was set up. It was officially registered on November 11 of that year, with offices at 231-233 Grand Buildings, Trafalgar Square, London. AE Morrison & Sons was joined as members by Electricars Ltd of Birmingham, the Young Accumulator Company of New Malden and Hants Electric Chassis. The latter was a small company which acted as Morrison-Electric agents and is believed to have been located in the Andover area. Each company continued operating at their individual locations but it wasn't long before Morrison's and Electricars began to work more closely. This led to eventual rationalisation of their respective ranges. Young Accumulator became Crompton Batteries Ltd,

with a factory in Newport, South Wales, while little is known of the fortunes of Hants Electric Chassis. The main players in Associated Electric Vehicle Manufacturers were Morrison and Electricars. The latter had been in the electric vehicle business for nearly two decades and had specialised in producing chassis to carry heavy loads, mainly for refuse collection. They also manufactured a separate, successful range of battery electric industrial trucks. Although they produced lightweight vehicles with payloads of between one and two tons, their product range in general was highly complementary to that of the Morrison-Electric stable. Perhaps it was no surprise therefore that a healthy relationship developed between the two companies.

TRANSATLANTIC TRADERS

Electricars was established in 1919 and operated from two areas of a factory site owned by the Birmingham Metal & Munitions Co. Ltd in Landor Street, Birmingham. The company began by acquiring electric road vehicles from America's Edison Manufacturing Company.

These formed the basis of the Electricars range for many years and as a result Edison maintained a close interest in the British company.

Early Electricars models were suited to heavy usage with payloads of up to six tons, something which proved popular with many local authorities. It wasn't long before vehicles suitable for smaller payloads were produced. They were aimed at payloads of a ton and above, and were fitted with small solid-tyred wheels.

Electricars suffered troubled times during the early 1920s but trade appears to have picked up as they were able to make the short move from Landor Street to new premises in Lawley Street during 1929. It is unclear exactly when the company began to produce battery electric industrial trucks, but a 1926 advertisement shows platform trucks with capacities of up to six tons and tow tractors able to haul loads of up to five tons. The company weathered the Great Depression of the early 1930s and was trading well when the amalgamation with AE Morrison & Sons took place in 1936. It is understood that Electricars moved to a new manufacturing base at Webb Lane, Hall Green, on the southern outskirts of Birmingham between 1938-39.

WAR AND PEACE

With their joint interests in mind in the 1930s, AE Morrison & Sons and Electricars started to look at their range of competing vehicles. At this time there appeared to be something of an identity crisis for the joint operation. In 1937, Associated Electric Vehicle Manufacturers published two leaflets, one sporting the Electricars banner, the other headlined Morrison-Electrics obviously referring to the ME range as the product title was actually presented in the singular. The leaflets were identical and showed only an Electricars one-ton chassis on the front cover. Inside there were colour photographs of early Morrison-Electric vehicles. Would-be buyers could be forgiven if they were confused by this.

Perhaps this had something to do with the fact that soon after, the one to two ton lightweight Electricars vehicles were phased out in favour of Morrison vehicles. However, the heavy duty Electricars vehicles – with payloads of two to six tons – continued in production through the Second

This mobile shop was typical of many supplied by the company. Complete with wheel spats the bodywork has been constructed on a one ton chassis.

World War. The last of these were produced in 1944 and assembled in Leicester. An interesting story told by George Morrison concerned a 30-seater battery electric bus built for the Guernsey Railway Company and delivered shortly before the outbreak of war in September 1939. The batteries for the vehicle were mounted, pannier fashion, between the wheels and accessed by means of side skirts secured by budget locks. The object was to change batteries halfway through each day to enable operation from early morning to later in the evening when the cinemas closed. The railway company had specified a road speed on the flat in excess of 23mph, but during a trial run with the police on board – to authorise the necessary road licence – it was pointed out that the maximum speed in the buses operating area was just 16mph. To comply with this ruling another rear axle differential was sent out from the factory to bring the road speed down. Unusually, internal fittings such as seats were supplied by the customer on this occasion. As the war progressed and as the Channel Islands fell under Nazi occupation nothing was heard of this electric vehicle. However, when hostilities ended, Guernsey Railway Company's transport manager wrote to Morrison-Electricar at Leicester, revealing that the occupying forces had broken up many of the island's buses, including the electric model.

The late 1930s were a busy time for AE Morrison & Sons along with other battery electric vehicle manufacturers. Indeed, by 1939 the year's output was nearly four times that of 1936. During the early war years Morrison's press advertisements carried the slogan: 'Seven out of every ten electric vehicles on the road are Morrison-Electricars.'

In 1941 Associated Electric Vehicle Manufacturers was taken over by Crompton Parkinson Ltd. An early action was to rationalise the range of lightweight vehicles into three payload capacities – 10cwt, 20cwt and 40cwt. The lighter Electricars range was phased out although the heavy payload vehicles were retained. In keeping with all other engineering companies the component AEVM enterprises were engaged in war work. They still manufactured electric vehicles in small quantities but the hoped for development and production rate did not materialise, due mainly to a shortage of raw materials.

As a result of the problems with manufacturing materials, the Ministry of Supply suggested to the Electric Vehicle Association of Great Britain that a standardisation sub-committee should be formed to prepare a specification for a standard battery electric chassis with a one-ton payload capacity. This would then have interchangeable components and could be manufactured by all electric vehicle companies. Although 1,000 vehicles were proposed, the scheme was never fully realised due to the ongoing shortage of materials, particularly rubber, and also Government restrictions on retail deliveries.

The 1930s and 40s brought some significant personnel changes at AE Morrison & Sons. In 1938 company founder AE Morrison retired. Just eight years later, in 1946, he died at the age of 69. In 1940, George Morrison left the company due to ill health and was transferred to other

This mobile shop, built on the CM 1 ton chassis delivered all manner of hardware products around the streets for its owners W. Adlam.

duties on the direction of the Government Employment Agency. Ultimately, he worked in the electric vehicle department of Loughborough's Brush Electrical Engineering. In 1941, AC Morrison left the business to become a consultant under contract to the Ministry of War. According to the May 1945 edition of the Electric Vehicles magazine, he set up a new battery electric vehicle manufacturing business - AC Morrison (Engineers) Ltd. of Leicester – with the product title ACM Douglas. It is understood that this business eventually moved to Bristol. AC Morrison died in July 1971.

In mid-1942 the AE Morrison & Sons product name changed from Morrison-Electric to Morrison Electricar to reflect its amalgamation with Electricars. A new badge was produced, featuring a wave design although many photographs of vehicles taken in 1943 still show the Morrison-Electric plate. Indeed, ME continued to advertise their vehicles in the trade press and sold them too! There are countless photographs of vehicles in use during the Second World War.

Another interesting event occurred in 1942 with the introduction of the route survey vehicle and battery calculation system. This was to have an impact on the use specific battery electric vehicles could be put to.

FIT FOR PURPOSE

Prospective buyers of battery electric vehicles were keen to know whether or not their power capacity was suitable for the tasks required of them. To ease any anxieties Morrison Electricar created a route survey form to establish a battery size suitable for a vehicle's duties.

For each route the first element to consider was the total weight of the load as the vehicle left the depot. The survey used the vehicle previously used to service a route, whether it was horse and cart, petrol engined or a BERV. Its driver would set out, followed by a car fitted with a gradient meter and with the mileometer set at zero. As the round continued, details of every delivery drop were recorded.

Also logged in the survey were every traffic stop, including traffic lights; the length in yards of every movement between stops; upward and downward gradients. It also recorded the amount of cargo left at each stop such as the number of milk bottles or loaves of bread. The type of road surface and an indication of any abnormal weather likely to be encountered were also factors that were taken into account.

Each completed survey was signed by the customer and returned to engineers at the factory. There they calculated the appropriate chassis type, axle ratio and size of battery for the route. If the order was for a vehicle due to tackle a new route, recommendations on model and battery would be worked out from information provided by the customer. Alternatively use of an appropriate demonstration BERV could be arranged. This would be fitted with an oversize battery to ensure it could accomplish its duties. When a vehicle was used for tasks which saw it leave the depot empty and return full, such as a refuse collection truck, details of the increasing load would be noted on the survey, along with all the other measurements. Some surveys found duties that were deemed too arduous for an electric vehicle, and the company would advise the would be customer accordingly and reluctantly, but respectfully decline to sell them one.

The route survey procedure may seem long-winded to today's commercial vehicle user, but it became a daily routine back then. The responsibility for the correct specification fell to the manufacturer, This avoided the possibility of wrongful selling, so the interests of both supplier and customer were well protected.

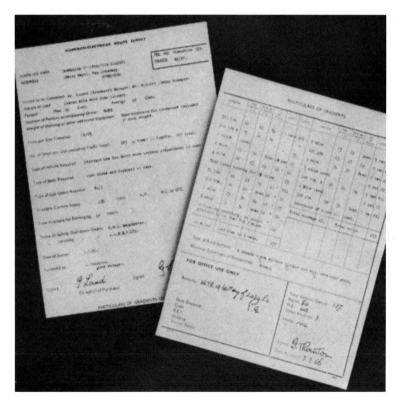

Route survey forms completed for one of the company's customers.

This vehicle shows just how versatile the electric chassis proved to be. Built on an E25 chassis, it is seen shortly after delivery in 1955 to a Leicester company who used it for inter-factory transport.

Two examples of early Morrison literature. On the left, a 1904 cycle and motorcycle catalogue alongside one for the company's Regalite air compressers.

A Trilec chassis bodied-up for a soft drink manufacturer in 1933. It couldn't have been the most comfortable vehicle for it's driver in inclement weather.

The ever popular BM model in the guise of a bakery van. It was supplied to, and operated by, the Co-operative Retail Society in South Wales.

CHALLENGES OF A NEW AGE

In 1946 a new range of vehicles was introduced, this time with letters signifying the model along with reference to its carrying capacity. The BM was 10 cwt, the CM one ton, the EM two tons and the GM three tons.

Internally, the company had a numbering sequence for each model which differed from that used by the sales department and recorded on their literature. This has caused confusion for many historians and without access to the vehicle build sheet – which showed both references – it is easy to see how this and errors in recognition have occurred. This book does not use internal references except in exceptional circumstances. Incidentally, it is understood that all works records were destroyed when the company's Tredegar, South Wales, factory closed in 1983.

Although Morrison-Electricar remained the dominant company with their road vehicles, the electric industrial truck side of Electricars continued to operate successfully from the firm's Birmingham factory. This enterprise,

under the title ITD Ltd – sometimes known as Industrial Truck Division but actually Industrial Truck Developments – had a sales operation centred at AEVM's London offices.

With the end of the austerity period after the war, it was a time for the company to look at new ways of promoting their products. When the Dairy Show restarted in 1948, at Olympia in London, this became the premier event for the company, catering for its largest market. The event was often used to introduce new models and, whenever possible, the vehicles would appear in the livery of a recognised fleet user.

For many the Dairy Show was seen as a great social occasion. Senior dairy trade figures would meet on the ME stand and friendships would be renewed between sales personnel, HQ staff and their clients. In October 1960 the show received royal patronage and was renamed the Royal Dairy Show. Indeed, in later years it reflected a growing foreign participation by taking the title Royal International Dairy Show. ME had taken display space at several shows before the war and at this time decided to particpate in more dairy-related exhibitions including the Bath & West Show which they took part in for several years. In February 1956 they exhibited for the first time at the Scottish Dairy Show in Glasgow's Kelvin Hall. It was a similar event to that in London and catered for the many ME users in Scotland. In later years the company also exhibited at the Commercial Motor Show, at Earls Court, London. Participation in exhibitions catering for other trades, such as bakery, and for the municipal market also featured in the company's marketing calendar.

The company also held its own regional demonstrations. A particularly important one took place in March 1947 at Heathrow Airport, London. The press reported a successful outcome although it is not known just how many sales were generated as a result. Three vehicles were on display, two one-ton factory CM demonstrators – one an enclosed van, the other with an open dairy body – and one BM, a10cwt van 'borrowed' from a London customer before delivery. The many guests at the event were given the opportunity to test-drive the demonstration vehicles. Far fewer aircraft used the airport at the time, but it is safe to say the demonstration runs were well away from even them.

In 1948 the Austin Motor Company of Longbridge, Birmingham, acquired a 50 per cent share in AEVM road vehicles. Shortly afterwards the company's name became Austin Crompton Parkinson Electric Vehicles Ltd (ACPEV). The sales office remained in London, with no change at the factory in Leicester. Export sales were transferred to Longbridge, however, where overseas markets were covered by the Austin Motor Export Corporation Ltd. A new badge was designed in the style of the existing Morrison-Electricar design. This read Austin-Electricar. Literature reflected this, doubtless as a means to capitalise on the Austin range well known to the worldwide market. This was the start of a successful period of co-operation between Austin and ACPEV that continued for over 20 years.

Although the company still used agents to sell their products in certain parts of the country, the sales department remained in London. With post-war expansion in the commercial motor industry, more sales staff were recruited and regular training sessions were held at the factory in Leicester. One 1946 photograph shows a temporary-style enclosure built in part of the main factory; it was used as the 'sales school' and would continue until a new office was built in the 1960s across the road.

The Electricars range of industrial trucks continued to sell well, operating as a separate entity to ACPEV. However, an announcement in the trade press of October 1949 revealed that the Austin Motor Company and Crompton Parkinson Ltd had, through their subsidiary company ACPEV Ltd, acquired control of ITD Ltd.

This was a strange announcement as Electricars industrial trucks had formed part of the company since 1936. A new range of forklift trucks was introduced alongside platform trucks, including the most successful model the TU20, and tow tractors. In 1957 the businesses of ITD and ACPEV separated completely and on January 1, 1962 the ITD name changed to Stacatruc Ltd. Around this time, America's Clark Equipment Company acquired a one-third share in Stacatruc and later it gained total control.

DECADE OF CHANGE

Two significant developments had an important bearing on events as the Morrison-Electricar business rolled through the 1950s. One was the introduction of two magazines. The first of these publications was titled Co-op & ME. It was aimed at the Co-operative movement, then one of the largest vehicle buying organisations in the UK. The magazine's content included details of ME vehicles supplied to Co-ops as well as features on Co-operative societies and the personnel running them.

A second new publication followed, this time titled You & ME. This was aimed at all other BERV users. These included large and small private dairies, laundries, local authorities, electricity supply companies and hospitals. The ME marketing team did a good job and the magazines were sent out to users and potential users for many years. They both continued until the mid-1960s by which time the marketplace had changed significantly. An attempt was made to relaunch Co-op & ME in 1968, but only two issues were printed. A few issues of You & ME were printed in a larger format in the early 1970s, but there seemed to be an overemphasis on sales-oriented material and the original editorial substance was lacking.

A pair of coal delivery vehicles supplied to Ipswich Co-operative Society in May 1951. Based on the GM three ton chassis with standard factory cabs and platform bodies. This photograph was taken in the society's coal yard and shows the vehicles being loaded prior to house-to-house deliveries. One of them remained in service until 1983, which illustrates the longevity of the electric vehicle chasis. The same vehicle is preserved in an Ipswich museum.

The second development saw the introduction of two new models at the Dairy Show in October 1952. A number of BERV manufacturers had enjoyed success in the dairy market by selling small, pedestrian controlled vehicles (PCV) for compact rounds. They were also useful for short, localised journeys in other environments such as hospitals and industrial sites. To break into this market ME introduced the P90 PCV. The P in this case stood for pedestrian, the 90 referred to the number of gallons of milk it could carry when used in the dairy trade. This model was available for a number of years, but sales were not high as well-established competitors had taken quite a lead in the market. Despite this limited success it was not the end of this humble pedestrian controlled vehicle's story.

The second vehicle launched at the 1952 Dairy Show was the MD30. This was a 30cwt chassis with a modern composite cab. While the majority of ME vehicles were delivered to the dairy trade, enclosed vans were available for other industries. According to literature printed early the following year, two sizes were offered in this style. These were the MD30 and the SD30. The initials MD stood for medium deck, for payloads of between 23 and 30cwt while SD stood for short' deck for payloads of between 22 and 28cwt. Demand for larger payload electric vehicles fell after this to a point where the company decided to abandon production of the three-ton GM vehicle.

In 1952 the Austin Motor Company became part of the British Motor Corporation. However, this didn't have any real effect on ACPEV and the relationship between Leicester and Birmingham continued.

The 1950s were a decade of real change, and at the October 1953 Dairy Show, another ME model was shown for the first time. Principally designed for the dairy trade and based on the MD chassis launched the

The front cover of a leaflet promoting ME vehicles for export. Overseas sales were dealt with by the Austin Motor Company, which explains why their name appears on it.

previous year, the MD20 and SD20 were rated with a capacity of 20cwt. The M again signified medium deck, with an internal length of 9ft 6in, and the S for short deck with an internal length of 7ft 11in. Each chassis was available for specialist bodywork such as vans and ambulances.

A BRILLIANT NEWCOMER

For many years the traditional method of manufacturing bodywork on commercial vehicles had meant the use of the composite system. This involved fabricating a wooden frame, creating the basic outline of the body, then attaching sheet metal to the frame. For certain applications, such as food transportation and hospital duties, another skin would be attached inside the body. The roof skin could either be metal or fabric attached to wooden parts of the frame. With the ever increasing cost of labour, this bodywork was expensive compared to that produced by other methods. To create a more competitive body, two new ME models were introduced in 1954. The D5 had a payload of up to 25cwt while the D4 had a capacity of up to one ton.

Introduced as 'a brilliant newcomer' and designed primarily for the dairy trade, the D5 came with a lightweight all-metal body on a welded steel tubular frame. This was easily detachable as a complete unit. The loading height of just 2ft 3½in was of benefit to the dairyman when lifting bottles and crates. It incorporated a removable central portion for access to the battery and the controller was repositioned under the driver's seat in a shortened cab. The model incorporated an interlock 'gate' ensuring the vehicle could not shift into reverse while moving forward and vice-versa. The controller was totally accessible for maintenance and could be removed for servicing by simply moving the driver's seat. In keeping with the theme of low cost, the electrical controller was basic to say the least: the accelerator foot pedal had two positions. When depressed halfway a mechanical contact engaged to give the first speed forward and, at the same time, an electrical 'hold-in' coil was engaged and held the first speed state. By moving the pedal, which had a small metal plate welded onto one side, slightly to the right and then depressing it, a second mechanical contact was made and the vehicle moved into second speed mode. Despite having just two speeds, forward and reverse, acceleration was not

This Truro Steam Laundry high roof line vehicle which was used to transport hanging garments is a good example of the flexibility of the D1 chassis.

A typical enclosed dairy body on the D1 chassis. This vehicle was part of the large Midland Counties Dairies fleet and is sporting a safety mirror above the windscreen.

jerky and proved satisfactory in service. Fitted with longer leaf springs mounted in Silentbloc bushes this improved the ride, with 11 inch Lockheed hydraulic brakes providing good stopping power. Despite its compact size, this model was still able to carry a 25cwt load. Its physical size and low initial cost proved advantageous not simply to the dairy trade as many photographs show it in use among countless different businesses.

The D4, again aimed at the dairy trade, was designed with a deck area to take 36 metal crates. When first announced it had a selling price of £580 for the complete vehicle minus battery and charger. This model, like its big brother the D5, proved ideal for the compact delivery round. However, it lacked facilities for carrying dairy products other than milk. The D4 was also fitted with a similar electrical controller to that of the D5.

Always on the lookout to reduce operating costs, many commercial vehicle operators would consider employing learner drivers who, on certain vehicles, could drive unaccompanied. This was important,

especially in the dairy trade, but irregularities in the law saw several learner drivers prosecuted, either because the vehicle's cab was fitted with two seats or the vehicle's weight was considered too great. In 1957, ACPEV met with the Ministry of Transport and representatives of the National Dairymens' Association to discuss their concerns. Accordingly, on October 1, 1957 a regulation was passed that learner drivers could drive an electric vehicle of 16cwt unladen weight and under and built to carry only one person in the cab unaccompanied. The D4 already met this requirement and the D5 could be supplied with a single seat to order.

Since the 1936 formation of AEVM and the 1941 takeover by Crompton Parkinson, the company had always had a London head office address, no doubt partly for prestigious reasons, but also because the sales force for both AEVM and ITD were based there. Sometime in 1950 there was a move to new premises at 95-99 Ladbroke Grove, W11. The company remained there for a few years but, because of the increasing customer

An atmospheric, post-war scene featuring the popular BM 10 cwt chassis with milk delivery body work, so familiar to many.

Ampere-hour meters like this were fitted to most ME vehicles until the early 1950's. A form of fuel guage, they indicated the amount of power remaining in the battery.

base in the Greater London area and the South-East, a search for larger premises began. The need was for a place where vehicles could be serviced, repaired and rebuilt.

The space situation was eased a little in 1957 when the sales forces moved, ACPEV staff to Leicester (although the PR department remained) and ITD staff to Birmingham. However, this did not solve the need for larger workshop space and the search continued for a new site. Finally, on December 1, 1958 the company moved to premises in Water Road on the Abbey Estate, off the North Circular Road in Wembley. The building had

originally been occupied by HM Stationery Office and had spread over an area of around 8,000 sq ft. The company had always been keen to promote the safety features on their vehicles, and several articles appeared in the trade press related to this aim. Among these was one describing a safety interlocking charging socket. This simple device consisted of a robust rod-type interlock between the direction-changing switch and a plate behind the charging socket, mounted to the side of the controller. The socket's flap cover could only be opened when the forward or reverse switch was in the neutral position and the hole in this plate mated

Just off the production line, this EH.20 has an all metal body, wind deflectors and a rear produce cupboard.

The BM model, complete with fully enclosed cab, in it's final, definitive form. This vehicle was supplied to a Cheltenham confectionery company.

with an arm on the flap, thereby allowing charging to take place. Most importantly, the vehicle could not be driven away whilst the plug and socket were still connected. Another device, used since the 1930s, was the ampere-hour meter. This consisted of a clock-type face with two pointers, one red, the other black. The red pointer was set at a battery discharged level equal to around 80 per cent discharge and the black at the fully charged rate. As the vehicle was used, the battery capacity would fall, the black pointer moving towards the red pointer and giving the driver an indication of how much battery capacity was available at any one time.

When the battery was recharged, the black pointer would return to the fully charged mark. This device became obsolete in the 1950s. In 1955 another safety device was introduced, the driver's safety view mirror. This ran the full width of the windscreen, mounted in a metal case above the glass. The mirror could be angled so the driver could see immediately in front of the vehicle, an area normally obscured from the driving position. The object was to see children who could be playing directly in front of the cab. The device was supplied to many customers on new vehicles and also for retro-fitting. With the introduction of glass fibre

A proud line-up of 10 cwt Morrison Electricar dairy vehicles outside the premises of G Cartwright & Son, Dunstable Road, Luton in June 1946.

Part of Cardiff Co-operative Society's milk delivery fleet. The vehicles were based on the D1 chassis.

The old and the new, in 1956. The last of the horse-drawn drays used by Staines Co-operative Society passes some of its fleet of new Morrison Electricar vehicles. They include an ED25 vehicle, two BM enclosed vans and four MD20 dairy vehicles.

A group of smart-suited salesmen employed by A&E Morrison & Sons at the sales school which was established in offices at the company's Brunswick works, Leicester on November 29, 1945.

bodies in the 1960s, this device was no longer necessary, due to the advent of larger windscreens and lower mounting.

Longevity has always been one of the most important sales features of the BERV, and although not so relevant in today's throwaway society, the cost saving to the user over the vehicle's lifespan was quite high when compared to that of an equivalent combustion engined vehicle. Indeed, manufacturers suggested a life expectancy of 15 to 20 years as normal for their electric vehicles, but many lasted even longer.

The 1936 trial in conjunction with a railway company of a three-wheeled electrically-powered mechanical horse was an idea that didn't reach full production, but the 1950s saw ME achieve greater success with a new four-wheel tractor unit, the GT. On May 19, 1949 the Daily Telegraph reported a statement made by Transport Commission chairman Sir Cyril Hurcomb at the annual luncheon of the Electric Vehicle Association.

He revealed that British Railways were carrying out trials with an electrically-powered mechanical horse which was expected to replace up to 7,000 horses used at the time for road transport deliveries. In 1949 British Railways ordered a tractor fitted with a very modern cab for trials at various locations. As a result of these trials in 16 cities and towns BR placed a large order for widespread evaluation purposes. By the early 1950s the delivery figure had become 142 units. These were located at depots across the Eastern, London Midland, North Eastern, Southern and Scottish regions. The tractor units carried loads of up to 2.5 tons, with a normal range of up to 25 miles per battery charge and a laden speed on the flat of 18mph. With a full load the vehicle was capable of climbing a gradient of one in nine. The prototype tractor unit has survived, fitted with a standard works cab, and is at the National Railway Museum in York. During their visits to customers, ACPEV staff were often told of really

A vehicle body displaying the company's patent forward safety mirror. It can be seen above the windscreen.

ancient vehicles that were still in use. This gave the marketing team the idea for a useful piece of public relations. A competition to find the oldest M-E or Electricar vehicle still in service was announced in the January 1960 issues of the magazines You & ME and Co-op & ME. The winners, one a Co-op member, one a non member, would each receive a prize of two guineas. The magazines carried a loose-leaf entry form for the competition. Vehicles over 20 years of age were shortlisted and of those, 14 entries came from Co-operative societies and 12 from others. The eldest was, fittingly perhaps, from Leicester. It was a 20 cwt Morrison Electric owned by Messrs W & F Goodman, a mobile fruit and vegetable business. Their vehicle, JF 8002, had been registered on March 20 1935 and was still in service at the time of the competition in 1960. Runner-up was an Electricar 15cwt dairy vehicle from Howards Dairies, of Westcliff-on-Sea, Essex. This had been registered on May 30, 1935. The winning entry in the Co-op section was GL 3497 registered on May 5, 1936. It was a 10cwt ME bread delivery van owned by Bath Co-operative Society. Runner-up was a 10/12cwt bread van registered on July 1, 1936 and owned by the Bristol Society. The Reading Society, incidentally, entered an Electricar dairy vehicle registered on the same day. Where these vehicles finally ended their days is unclear.

THE WEIGHT LIFTERS

The unavailability of a heavy load-carrying chassis must have been a problem at times. However, ME were not prepared to lose business because of that. So when, in 1960, they had an enquiry from the John Lewis Partnership in London for four large box vans, the engineering staff at Leicester got to work. John Lewis had bought Electricar 50cwt box vans before the war so it was perhaps because of their satisfaction with them that this new enquiry materialised. With no chassis suitable in their current range, an Austin three ton internal combustion-engined commercial chassis with a wheelbase of 12ft 1in was chosen to be electrified. Special bodywork, supplied by Marshall's (Cambridge) Ltd, was built on each chassis. After delivery to London, the vehicles were used to transport furniture and large goods from a Chelsea warehouse to the company's West End store. Goods bought by customers were then

The D4 chassis was very adaptable. This vehicle, seen in the late 1950s, was used at South Ockendon Hospital, Essex, for collection and delivery of laundry and additional duties including refuse disposal. It was supplied and bodied by F G Smith (Motors) Ltd. The extended deck, covered with Dural plate had an enclosed rear end, and featured detachable tubular steel centre and side pillars, to support its canvas hood and side curtains with retaining chains.The cab was of a special design with fully glazed doors and was adapted to seat two people. This was one of two similar vehicles supplied at the same time. The other had a totally enclosed body for distribution of food containers.

The three-quarter height rear cupboard on this glass fibre-bodied EH20 chassis was an optional extra. Many customers found it a useful addition.

taken to the warehouse for eventual onward delivery and it was during this process that these vehicles enjoyed a unique use. At the store an ME vehicle would be driven from the street into the goods entrance, then taken to the basement on a large goods lift. It would be driven onto a turntable built into the floor, allowing it to be positioned for manoeuvring towards a loading dock. The low height of each van was crucial because of the limited basement height. The process would be reversed when each vehicle left the store. Benefits to the retailer included an avoidance of street parking needs in a heavily congested area, the use of load-bearing

vehicles in confined indoor areas and, of course, virtually silent, fume free operation. MEs were supplied in standard format to this prestigious customer in the succeeding years. This wasn't the only time a non-BERV chassis was 'electrified' though.

The company had always been keen to welcome visitors to their factory in South Wigston, but for many customers distance precluded a personal visit. With this in mind in late 1957 a photo shoot was arranged and many shots of the company's various departments were taken. They showed the production process and were featured in the January 1958 issues of house magazines, Co-op & ME and You & ME. An article on the same theme also appeared in Electric Vehicles magazine two months later. The demand for battery electric vehicles never reached such a level that mass production could be considered, so a batch production system operated. This had the advantage of flexibility as a vehicle could be tailored to meet any customer's demanding variations at an economical

A GT model tractor and trailer unit in cream and maroon British Railways livery.

price and without disturbance to the production line. As the 1950s neared their end, up popped another new model. In mid-1958, the company announced the EH20 chassis, effectively an update of D5 model. New features included a restyled cab with wind deflectors as standard and doors available as an optional extra. Higher road speeds were possible due to an increased number of cells in the battery. Under the driver's seat there was an automatic speed control using three electro-mechanical contactors operated by a pneumatic time delay footswitch similar to that on the larger D1 chassis. There was also a single action footswitch in place of the old two-position pedal. With its larger battery the vehicle was capable of a laden level road speed of around 14mph, allowing operators to plan longer rounds with a possible payload of 25cwt.

Just as the 1950s proved to be a decade of change, the 1960s also brought new models and variations. In 1960 the EH/F20 appeared, with a cab and canopy specifically for dairy trade. This was made of fibreglass laminate. Announced at the Dairy Show that year, it featured the EH20 chassis with a one-piece, moulded cab, semi-flexibly mounted on the chassis. A wraparound front gave a fair degree of weather protection and the glazing gave a high level of vision to the side and front. Cab doors were available as an optional extra. A fibreglass fascia board was moulded into the cab front incorporating driving instruments and providing a convenient writing area, with an integral book pocket. The two bench seats were covered with relatively comfortable upholstery and had a matching backrest. The electrical switchgear remained under the driver's

Workmen at the Brunswick Works, Leicester, apply finishing touches and final adjustments before a number of completed vehicles leave for delivery to some of Morrison's customers during late 1957. They are, from the left: a BM 10cwt chassis with dairy body; an E25 flat deck body; a D4 with single headlamp and the cab of a MD one-tonner.

seat, but the pneumatic delay footswitch was moved to the front with the accelerator pedal attached. For the first time, three separate windows were fitted into the rear of the cab, providing improved vision.

Although announced as a new model with all the attendant fanfare, a list of vehicle exhibits published before the 1959 Dairy Show had referred to an EH20 with a newly-styled fibreglass cab. It was said to be of 'outstanding interest'. Moreover, the company's list of vehicles for exhibition at the 1960 show referred back to the previous year and the EH20 that had been displayed then. The explanation was that the 1959 model had been a prototype, a preview of what was to come. Following the usual trait of changing the model reference according to specification

changes, this model was variously known as the E25F, EH20cwt, EH/F20 and finally the reference it retained until the end, the EH20F.

The following year, 1961, witnessed a number of acquisitions by ACPEV. The first of these was that of the entire electric vehicle interests of TH Lewis Ltd, of Watford. This firm had been making BERVs since before the Second World War and was closely associated with London's Express Dairy Company which had financial interests in the company. There were two models in particular which were retained. These were the Electruk Rider, in which the operator could either drive while standing or sitting on a high bench seat, and the Electruk pedestrian operated model. Both became part of the ME range, the former as the E15 and the PCV as the DPC3. The original ME pedestrian controlled model, the P90, had

Clean lines and extra visibility typified Morrison's EH20 chassis. This glass fibre-bodied vehicle had a 15 crate per tier deck.

Employees at work attaching wiring looms to a line-up of chassis at the Leicester factory during 1957.

been discontinued by this time. Express Dairy continued to purchase the E15 for several years, having built up quite a fleet of them when they were built by TH Lewis. Indeed, when the model was shown for the first time, on the ME stand at the 1961 Royal Dairy Show it was in Express Dairy fleet colours. The London Co-operative Society were also large users of this model. The standard E15 used mechanical contactors giving it three speeds, two with batteries in parallel and one with batteries in series. Alternatively, a carbon stack controller was available at extra cost. This gave a smoother acceleration by compressing carbon discs hydraulically using footswitch pressure.

From the start of electric vehicle production in 1933 the 10/12 cwt payload chassis became the most popular in terms of sales. It continued in use for many years with various specification changes. The model eventually became known as the BM chassis. In the 1950s, with the introduction of metal framed bodywork on the D4 and D5 models and later use of glass fibre bodies, demand for the BM chassis with composite metal clad, wooden framed bodywork declined. This type of bodywork

was generally only specified when customers requested a specialised vehicle such as an ambulance with walk through facility from the cab into the rear body.

Following the factory move to Tredegar and the loss of staff familiar with composite body construction, sales of this chassis finally ended in 1968 with the final two vehicles produced being mobile canteens for the Ministry of Defence. The final model BM60 had different wheel frames as the earlier pattern pressed-disc wheels were no longer available. So ended a chassis run of 35 years which must be one of the longest from any commercial vehicle manufacturer.

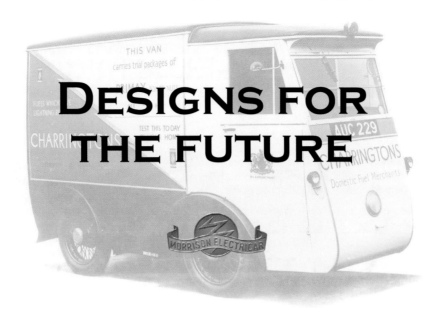

DESIGNS FOR THE FUTURE

As demand for ME products increased during the early 1960s, plans were drawn up to build an office block on a new site in Countesthorpe Road, across the road from the main Leicestershire factory.

In July 1957, when the industrial truck business had been separated from the road vehicle side, the sales and administration team had been re-formed in Leicester. Temporary office space was made available in the factory but this was not a satisfactory situation. Work on the new building started in late 1962 with completion scheduled for February the following year. The building, on three levels, had a floor area of 10,500sq ft with accommodation for sales and office staff as well as design and drawing office accommodation on the first two floors. On the top floor there was a kitchen and canteen. Service and parts administration staff were located on the ground floor. When the building was completed and staff moved in, the former offices were removed and the space made available for production work.

In 1963 the company changed the badge on the front of each cab and implemented a new design. Smaller and simpler, it could be produced at lower cost. Out went the well-known pressed metal wave design, in came an almost square, slightly oval, two-tone blue badge bearing the words Morrison-Electricar.

On most commercial vehicles, cab doors had hinges fitted to the front corner pillar. While these proved adequate for most applications, the process of getting in and out could become tiresome on vehicles designed for multiple stop-start duties, where doors could be opened up to 300 times a day. The opening doors were also not without danger to the driver, pedestrians and other road users. In most cases, electric vehicles used for milk deliveries had no doors, mainly due to the number of times personnel were required to enter and exit their cab. In late 1962, the Kidderminster Co-operative Society's transport manager began experimenting on his ME dairy vehicles by fitting sliding doors on one side of the cab and jack-knife doors on the other. At the end of the experiments, it was agreed that all their vehicles would be fitted with jack-knife doors. The society approached ACPEV and asked if they would supply their new vehicles with such features and this was agreed. The standard vehicle supplied to Kidderminster Co-op was the D1 with composite body. On new vehicles the company now modified the cab slightly to fit a bi-fold door. The first two vehicles delivered with these doors were believed to be the first battery electric vehicles of their kind in Britain. This door challenge was taken seriously at the ME factory and the solution was found by engineering staff who devised an ingenious idea to fit cab doors. Photographs still show bi-fold doors fitted on vehicles supplied to other customers, on the larger composite bodied chassis and particularly for non-dairy users.

Smoother progress

In early 1963, ACPEV announced that after extensive trials they were able to offer customers the option of an electronic controller instead of the traditional electrical controller which utilised electro-mechanical contactors and a large grid resistance. The new device, the Powermiser, was developed and patented by Electro-Voice Products Ltd who arranged with ACPEV to supply the units for new vehicle orders, for the conversion of orders that were going through the factory at the time and for retro-fitting on vehicles recently supplied.

The Powermiser offered some attractive features and many benefits to the user. For a start, it had no moving parts so there would be a saving on maintenance. Periodic attention to the contactors on the old system had been a regular part of the maintenance schedule. Speed control was step-less, avoiding jerky movements and resulting in the removal of strain on the transmission system and the problem of half-shaft breakage. In fact a driver could put his or her foot hard down on the accelerator pedal and the vehicle would still move off at a controlled speed. With this ultra-smooth acceleration it was possible to hold the vehicle on a gradient with no time limitation at low speed running, similar to the automatic gearbox on a modern car or slipping the clutch on a manual gearbox. Also, there was now the ability to operate under any battery voltage condition, with built-in automatic protection for the controller. An undoubted saving in battery consumption could be demonstrated as there was no power wastage due to the elimination of the resistance grid. The system used semi-conductors, sometimes known as thyristors, an electronic switch with no moving parts which would send pulses of voltage to the motor at micro-second intervals. A pulse generator read would provide the frequency and length of pulses, depending on the position of the foot switch. As the vehicle speed increased

The factory at Tredegar, South Wales, seen from the air soon after its illuminated roof sign was changed to read Crompton Electricars.

each pulse would remain on for longer until, at full road speed, the pulses would end and full battery voltage would be applied to the motor. If an overload condition existed – for example, if the payload was too great or the driver set off with the handbrake on – a protection device would activate, stopping further motion until the overload had been removed. In technical journals and ME's own magazines, these features were promoted as bringing many positive benefits. However, initially there was a higher price. These were early days for electronic controllers on road-going vehicles and the small number of units sold added to the costs as did the relative sparsity of individual electronic components. In the years to follow, a greater acceptance of this type of controller resulted in a lower cost to the vehicle builder.

WINNING WAYS

Following success with glass fibre bodies on the EH/20F chassis, an increased demand for this type of bodywork became evident for the heavier payload vehicles too, especially as their manufacture would reduce labour costs associated with construction of composite bodies. On the ME stand at the October 1963 Royal Dairy Show, there appeared a scale model of the proposed new fibreglass bodywork to be fitted to all future D and F models. Primarily of interest to the dairy trade, this cab gave more visibility to the driver through a large curved windscreen. There was a lower entry step into the cab and better visibility to the rear through three glazed panels similar to the EH20F. Use was not confined to the dairy trade however. Many vehicles were supplied direct to the customer in chassis and cab form or alternatively direct to their own body builder for box van bodies and in particular ambulance bodies to be fitted. Most importantly, the cab was designed with a solution to the old door problem.

Early in 1964 the D1's first glass fibre body was announced and a new type of cab door displayed. This innovative, patented design was to prove a real winner for the company. Running on top and bottom tracks, the doors would slide in front of the windscreen - inside the cab - when opened, and could be closed by means of a slam lock. Gone were hinged doors and the problem of constantly opening them at the risk of accident.

A close view of new glass fibre cab on a D36/25 chassis showing inner glide door.

This dust cart shows just one of the many uses that local authorities found for electrically powered vehicles.

As it was possible to see through the door and windscreen at the same time, the new glide-in doors could be left in the open position if the driver was on a part of his round which necessitated constant getting in and out of his cab. The opportunity was given to change the model designation and the first model carried the D/Fg mark. Although the company openly referred to the use of 'fibreglass' in the construction of its cabs and the deck canopy when offered to the dairy trade, use of the word was incorrect as Fibreglass was a registered trademark. Although there seems to have been no deliberate trademark infringement of this, or any attempt to intervene by the Fibreglass Company, efforts were made in-house to use the description 'glass fibre'. The trade press, not wishing to become involved perhaps, used the two word title 'fibre glass'. When the new vehicles were displayed at 1964's Royal Dairy Show the company won the top award of a silver medal in the inventions competition.

An important advantage of glass fibre was the fact that colour impregnation using a variety of colours was possible. Customers could choose their own fleet colours without the need to spray paint them. Of course, the cab and canopy could be sprayed if necessary. Not surprisingly for the dairy trade, the colour in greatest demand was broken white.

The March 1965 edition of Electric Vehicles magazine brought advance reports of the new, smaller Morrison-Electricar vehicle. This would replace the old D5, EH20 and EH20F chassis and would incorporate a new cab design with inner-glide doors. The opportunity was given to issue new model designations, and these became the E/Fg16 (works reference D6-G), the E/Fg 24 (D6-K) and the E/Fg 30 (D6-L) chassis. The figures following E/Fg in each case referred to the number of cells in the battery. The chassis remained basically the same as those of the previous models although there was a slight increase at the front to allow for the operation of the new doors. The tyre specification was upgraded to 23 x 5 10 ply and a new 300amp charge/run plug became the standard. The old three-pin charge plug with mechanical interlock was discontinued, the new type enabling the plug from the charger to mate with a socket on the side of the control panel with a locking handle after the run plug had been disconnected. The principal safety feature of being unable to drive off while on charge, was maintained without the need for special interlocks. Because of the new door, specifically the bottom runner, it was no longer possible to include the old-style pneumatic delay footswitch, hence the accelerator pedal was mechanically linked to the controller which was still mounted under the driver's seat.

Despite availability of the electronic controller, most customers preferred the older system of using electro-mechanical contactors in conjunction with a grid resistance so time-delay switches on the contactors gave the necessary speed acceleration. The E/Fg 16 had two contactors, the E/Fg 24 three and the E/Fg 30 four. At the top of the new cab a flat moulded panel was incorporated, principally intended for a number plate although some customers used the space for their name or an advertisement. The canopy on dairy models incorporated moulded grooves which gave excellent rigidity and rain-drain facility. A wooden rear bumper was standard, and later, due to the vulnerability of the cab's lower edge, a metal bumper became available for the front.

An interesting vehicle was displayed on the ME stand at the 1963 Royal Dairy Show. It had one door which didn't open to the outside of the cab.

The 3K2, three-wheeled milk delivery vehicle. This one was delivered to Metcalfe's Dairies.

Many dairies now realised that customers wanted a range of products in addition to milk so they were looking at ways of carrying these products. Mobile shops had of course already been carrying a range of goods for a number of years. An electric vehicle chassis is versatile in that it allows a vehicle's specification to be adapted for customer-requested modifications. Most dairy trade requests were for the provision of goods boxes to carry dairy products other than milk. These could be fitted behind the cab or under the rear deck.

One revolutionary design came from the Unigate Group's South Coast Dairies Ltd, based in the Brighton and Hove area. Their transport manager, Mr Gunner, adapted a Morrison vehicle and had a new body built with a large cab incorporating a display and storage area behind the driver and passenger. Bread, groceries and dairy products were stored there and displayed through the rear windows. Entry to the cab was from behind, through a sliding door with a walkway between the cab and milk-carrying deck. The drive motor was mounted behind the rear axle, along with the control panel and resistance grid. The deck could be hinged upwards and propped up allowing excellent access to these components. The canopy extended over the deck in a cantilever fashion without the need for rear pillars.

Later, ACPEV were asked to build a new chassis with these modifications, and Unigate subsidiary, Wincanton Transport & Engineering Ltd, built the body. This vehicle was called the Gunner.

The chassis used was the F30, an up-rated version of the D1. However, demand for this design did not materialise, possibly due to the higher price of both modified chassis and body. It is also possible that, with the success of the new standard glass fibre models with inner-glide doors and the ability to fit a variety of goods boxes, ME did not want to pursue the Gunner-style design.

When the ACPEV sales manager left the company in 1968 to join their main competitor, his new employer quickly launched a new vehicle range incorporating a body design that featured many Gunner innovations.

THREE-WHEEL REVIVAL

In 1965, Express Dairies Ltd asked ACPEV to design and produce a three-wheel dairy delivery vehicle. A competitor had successfully produced mainly three-wheel chassis for many years. Two chassis sizes were planned, similar in specification to the E/Fg and F/Fg four-wheel models but with a Scammell single front wheel unit. The model designations were to be known as 3D6-G and 3F11 respectively. On the smaller unit, the E/Fg cab could be simply modified to take the front wheel unit. However, cabs for the larger model were built by Mickleover Transport Ltd. Standard three or four stage contactor control was specified, with the Powermiser an optional extra. Cab doors would not be available on either model. A number of these chassis were built, including some for non-dairy customers who required van bodywork. On display at the 1966 Commercial Motor Show was a 3F11 with a van body from Mickleover for Betabake Bakeries..

The New Year of 1966 saw the announcement of another new model to the range. It was one of the smallest machines ever produced by the company. The Midge was a personnel runabout for interworks and off-road use. It featured a single moulded glass fibre body incorporating bonded-in metal structures to accommodate the wheel assemblies. A seat took two people, albeit rather intimately. The Midge came in two basic models. These were the R1-A single-speed and the R1-B twin-speed. The 1.5hp motor was powered by heavy-duty industrial pattern batteries of either 12V or 24V. A small 240V charger was fitted into the boot and incorporated an automatic cut-out device, allowing for charging to take place at any convenient mains socket. Drive consisted of a two-stage reduction with the motor driving through toothed pulleys and a belt, with a chain final drive. An automatic clutch was incorporated to control torque. When the sales brochure arrived, a planned colour choice of red, blue or green had changed to red, white or yellow.

From July 4-9, 1966, the company exhibited at their first overseas show, the Munich Dairy Congress in Germany. Two vehicles were displayed, an F/Fg in the colours of the Express Dairy Company and the smaller E/Fg in the colours of the CWS Milk Division. According to Electric Vehicles magazine, the firm's management was pleased with the number of visitors to their stand and with the interest shown in the cabs and their inner-glide doors. In late 1966, at the Dairy Show, another new model was unveiled. The 3K2 was based on the 3F11 chassis introduced the previous year. The new model, with a futuristic glass fibre cab giving a 180 degree arc of vision to the driver, had shelves fitted behind the cab for groceries and dairy products.

A key advance was the front steering system. No longer a Scammell unit, it was newly designed, mounted on a turntable and operated by a chain going around the periphery of the turntable. Because of the circular frontal design, no doors were fitted. However, the operator could conveniently handle crates from the front edges of the deck whilst exiting the cab. Another interesting feature was the Gainmaster booster unit. Its aim was to increase the range of the vehicle when normal batteries would not be large enough to cover an entire round. The Gainmaster was a generator under the deck at the rear and powered by a Calor propane gas cylinder mounted nearby. The prototype was sold to Metcalfe's Dairy, but it doesn't appear that this vehicle went into production. It is not known whether or not the Gainmaster was sold to other BERV users. Early 1967

saw the introduction of a new reed-type foot switch. This consisted of an inner and outer cylindrical moulding of black plastic, the outer moving down the inner. When pressed down a series of reed switches were activated by magnets, which then passed a voltage to each contactor in turn. Time delay mechanisms were still mounted on each of these. As the reed switches were sealed in glass there would be no effect from water or damp intrusion. The outer part of the assembly was spring-loaded to return to its original position. The main advantage was simplicity of fitting without the need for mechanical linkages. The device also removed any possible obstruction to the sliding door track on the driver's side. It was stated by the manufacturers that the switch would operate many millions of times before any replacement was necessary, therefore making it virtually maintenance free. In service however, it was not as successful as envisaged. The plastic case was vulnerable to mechanical damage caused by the driver's boot!

In 1968 the company brought out a BERV distributor in the Midlands, the first acquisition of many in the years ahead. Electric Vehicle Service (Birmingham) Ltd had been established in the city's Nechells area for many years and run by a brother and sister of the Treece family. Their father JW Treece had enjoyed connections with the former Electricars company and had been a director of AE Morrison & Sons in the early days. The Treece business continued to operate as a separate entity until early 1974 when Crompton Electricars Ltd opened a new depot in the Birmingham area. As we know, ACPEV model designations were complicated due to reference differences between sales and works teams. No more was this so than with the D1 with its semi-floating rear axle and capacity of up to 30cwt, although the payload could be increased to 32cwt with a smaller battery specification. At the higher payload end during the old composite bodied days, the model became known as the F Model, and when glass fibre cabs came along we saw reference to the D/Fg (21/26cwt) and F/Fg (30/32cwt) models. However, it wasn't until the last few years of the 1960s when a fully floating rear axle was introduced heralding the F/Fg model proper, a designation it retained until the end of the business, ultimately replacing the old D model with the end of the semi-floating axles.

THE QUEST FOR SPACE

During the late 1960s, it became apparent that insufficient production space at the Leicester works was affecting the manufacture of electric vehicles, especially at a time when order books were full and the future for BERV's was assured.

The company considered options including expansion at South Wigston, and the building of a new factory elsewhere in Leicester. Expansion was a non-starter as the factory was in a heavily populated area. A cross-town move was vetoed by the Board of Trade due to the area's limited availability of skilled labour. However, the Board offered to build a new factory for the firm in a development area, with several sites suggested. The ACPEV board agreed to a new-build in Tredegar, South Wales and on February 1, 1967, work started on the factory at the town's Dukestown Industrial Estate.

Designed as an electric vehicle production facility, the factory covered 82,000sq ft and cost £450,000. It provided a production facility for up to 2,500 vehicles per year. A roadway of around a third of a mile was laid around the building and several inclines were built into it at set gradient levels to provide a vehicle test track. In the plant's basement was a design and development department where many future vehicles would first see light. In September 1967, a small production area was set up manufacturing vehicles and providing training facilities for locally recruited labour. The first vehicle built completely at Tredegar left the works in April 1968. By the end of October that year the South Wigston factory had closed. This brought to an end 35 years of electric vehicle production in Leicester. Many key staff at Leicester, having made several visits to Tredegar, decided to move there.

The new facility created much interest in the local and national media and it was fitting that an official unveiling was arranged. On October 11, 1968 Welsh Secretary George Thomas duly performed the opening ceremony. The London-based public relations department of Crompton Parkinson organised media activity and their Longbridge-based BMC counterparts dealt with photographic and film arrangements, while I co-ordinated the event. It featured an opening address by ACPEV acting chairman Mr EW Pedlow who briefly detailed the company's history. He introduced George Thomas who gave encouragement to the new business before declaring the factory officially open.

A cavalcade of the company's products followed, possibly the only time such an array of electric vehicles with such diverse duties had ever been gathered together. First in the parade was the company's northern area sales manager and the day's master of ceremonies. Driving a Midge personnel carrier he introduced each vehicle as it drove around the factory which had been cleared for the day.

Each vehicle, with two exceptions, had recently been built for customers whose permission had been obtained to display them. Indeed, several had already entered service and had been returned to the factory especially for the day. The vehicles were:

- A PCV, model DPC3 with a flat-deck body, owned by Prudential Assurance.

- An E/Fg standard medium range dairy model, owned by the Unigate Group's Lovells Creameries.

- A two-ton capacity F36/40 full-range milk delivery vehicle, owned by London's Express Dairy.

- A special bakery and confectionary delivery van based on a D36/25 chassis and owned by CWS Motor Trade. This was brought to Tredegar directly from Bristol shortly after completion, before entering service.

- A parcel delivery van based on a D36/25 chassis and loaned by the GPO. It had been built in Leicester and supplied the previous year.

- A special open-bodied personnel carrier owned by ICI for use at a salt mine in Winsford, Cheshire. This was based on the D36/25 chassis.

- A mobile butchery shop recently built on a FL36/40 long wheelbase chassis and bought by the Wellingborough Co-operative Society.

- A special medical research mobile laboratory recently displayed on the company's stand at the Commercial Motor Show. Based in Edinburgh

An Electruk Rider E15 Model with an unpainted standard alloy dairy body. The longitudinal display board was an optional extra.

and built on a FL36/40 chassis, it was loaned to the official opening by the Medical Research Council.

- The company's refuse collection demonstrator – on a D36/25 chassis - with a three cubic yard capacity Derby-type body incorporating hydraulics for end tipping.

- A demonstrator on the F36/40 chassis and mounting a Skyworker hydraulic aerial lift incorporating a double-cage platform.

- One of two 25-seat buses ordered by the Electricity Council for use at the National Agricultural Centre in Stoneleigh, Warwickshire. Mounted on the FL36/40 chassis, it was fitted with a Powermiser controller.

- A vehicle mounted on an old M-E chassis, but with a new, specially armoured body, built by owners Express Dairy. This unique vehicle was used to deliver cash wages to staff.

A typical hospital internal ambulance built on an F/Fg36/35 chassis. This vehicle is displaying the new style badge on the cab front just below the windscreen.

Incidentally, the models available in 1968 included the D36/25 - basically the old D1 model with glass fibre bodywork, the F/Fg range offering payloads up to two tons, the three E/Fg chassis, the E15 Rider, the DPC3 pedestrian chassis and the faithful old BM60 Mk2 chassis for those customers requiring a lightweight vehicle with composite bodywork.

The majority of these vehicles were fitted with a single front headlight, common practice on slow moving road vehicles. However, this was to change in 1968 when new regulations required that all four-wheel vehicles had two headlights. The ruling stated that all vehicles built on and after April 1, 1968 must comply and that their headlight positioning was defined. Through the Electric Vehicle Association, strong representations were made to the Government for a BERV exemption and these were partially successful. The new requirement was for all BERVs built after

October 1, 1969 to have twin headlights, with older vehicles to comply by October 1, 1971 if capable of exceeding 15mph on the level or by October 1, 1973 if not capable of exceeding 15mph on the level.

THE NAME GAME

In 1969, the company's official title changed. This was to be the first of several rapid changes, including a number of acquisitions. One significant change had already taken place when, on January 1, 1967, the old company name of AE Morrison & Sons, up until then still retained as a registered name, was changed to Morrison-Electricar Service Ltd. This name fronted a new division of the company, responsible for all servicing and spare parts supply. In 1969, a merger took place between the British Motor Corporation and Leyland Motors, and the 50 per cent ME share held by the Austin Motor Company went to them. As a result, the electric vehicle business became known as Crompton Leyland Electricars Ltd (CLE). In 1972, the British Leyland Motor Corporation sold its share to the Hawker Siddeley Group, parent company of Crompton Parkinson and CLE. The new company name was Crompton Electricars Ltd. At this time Hawker Siddeley also owned other companies involved in electric vehicle manufacture – Loughborough's Brush Electrical Engineering, RA Lister & Co of Dursley, Gloucestershire, and Brook Victor Electric Vehicles of Huddersfield, Yorkshire.

It was apparent that Hawker Siddeley was anxious to amalgamate their electric vehicle manufacturing interests, and in late 1969 manufacture of Brush industrial trucks was transferred to Tredegar. This was a good move, as the quality Brush models were good sellers and this presented many new opportunities for CLE. Almost all the vehicle designs involved in the transfer were industrial trucks, with the exception of the Brush Pony three-wheeler which was suitable for highway use and was illustrated in company literature for some time. Indeed, several were produced in the years that followed. One big seller was the SD tractor and a similar range of platform trucks, incorporating the drive unit originally designed by AC Morrison back in 1940.

Staff look on as a pedestrian controled flat-bed truck passes by during the vehicle parade that was part of the official opening of the Tredegar factory.

An employee puts one of the Brush industrial trucks that were built at Tredegar through its paces during a test run around the factory.

SHOWING THE WAY

An entirely new vehicle was launched on the ME stand at the Commercial Motor Show in September 1970. It represented a complete departure from the traditional road-going chassis of previous models. The A1 van, or pick-up, was designed at the Tredegar factory and marketed as suitable for deliveries of light goods for a wide variety of trades. The chassis was formed of robust steel square section with an angled steel frame for the battery box. The front drive axle was a modification of the Austin Mini unit, supplied by a parent company, and the rear sub-frame came from the same source. Drive to the front wheels was by way of two series-wound motors, each rated at 3.9hp and force-ventilated by two external blower fans. Control was achieved through a carbon stack device and then electro-mechanical contactors arranging the motors in series or parallel depending on the speed requirement. Depression of the foot pedal initially gave first speed; a second depression and operation of a push button gave final speed. The battery of 24 cells, made up of eight semi-traction monoblock batteries with three cells per battery, provided a 48V supply. The battery charger was built into the chassis, with a 25ft trailing lead and a 13A plug which allowed for recharging from any convenient mains supply. The Austin Mini wheels were fitted with radial ply tyres. Bodywork, constructed from glass fibre reinforced plastic, came in two sections. These were the front cab scuttle and doors fixed to the chassis, and the cab roof and rear bodywork which was hinged at the rear and could be lifted for access to all the components underneath. The bodywork incorporated indents and ridges for rigidity and could be impregnated with a colour of the customer's choice. The vehicle was designed to carry a 500lb payload with a level running speed of up to 33mph and a range of 25 miles. Hawker Siddeley was anxious to see sales at home and abroad and several did indeed go overseas.

It's possible that some design elements had originated from the manufacture of a two-seat electric car requested by British Leyland Motor Holdings chairman Lord Stokes in late 1969. The car used Austin Mini components from Longbridge and is believed to have been built in Tredegar. It is understood that this car survives in a museum.

During the early 1970s CLE were concerned at the success of the rear-entry cab design of their principal competitor. Their strategy was to highlight the advantages of their own cab design on the E and F models, with the inner-glide doors, and how easy it was to enter and exit the cab with its single step. However, under pressure from the sales force, the company also produced its own rear-entry cab. The Commando, announced in 1971, was broadly based on the F chassis but due to it being forward control, without the front step-down frame. It was known as the K range and there were two models - the K36/75 to take up to 165 gallons of milk and the K36/85 for 220 gallons. The first figures in each designation referred to the number of cells in the battery, the second figure referred to the maximum gross vehicle weight, 75cwt and 85cwt. The bodywork, all glass fibre including the deck area canopy if used for milk deliveries, had a cab comprising of four sections in addition to the roof. The object of this design was to easily replace individual panels after accident damage. It avoided major surgery to the whole cab area. This was particularly pertinent with regard to the lower panel at the front of the cab. Customers had remarked on the cost of repairs to glass fibre cabs as a result of accident damage to the front. With so many replaceable panels it is possible cab rigidity was compromised so this facility was

One of two midi-buses ordered by the Department of Industry for inner-city trials.

later dropped. The whole canopy structure was a one-piece moulding, extending over to form the cab's roof.

The dairy version was well received so another version aimed specifically at the municipal market was unveiled in 1972. This was the Commando Street Tidy. It used the K36/85 chassis and had a five-man crew cab. Rear entry and exit was provided to the nearside only. The equivalent offside area was used to accommodate a wet clothes locker. A wash hand basin and crew food storage area was also provided. The rear steel bodywork was of the traditional Derby type for general refuse collection with a capacity of 3.9cu yd on a standard chassis and 5.25cu yd on the long wheelbase version.

A further acquisition came in 1972 when one of the company's most successful agents, Transport Electrics Ltd, was bought. Apart from their headquarters in Bristol they had a depot in Plymouth, which subsequently

A milk delivery vehicle on the K-type chassis with an early sectioned cab.

became CE's service centre for Devon and Cornwall. Other changes came in 1973 when the product title became Crompton Electricars, with the famous hyphen taken away. For many people this was a sad move; no longer would the product carry the Morrison name which the vehicles had displayed since 1933.

A TESTING TICKET

Decline in the sales of traditional BERVs, mainly those to the dairy trade, were now beginning to show so the early 1970s brought plans to diversify into other markets. The company were approached by the Department of Industry to manufacture two battery electric single-deck buses which would be loaned to fleet operators for evaluation purposes. The original idea had emanated from Leeds City Transport (LCT) who were seriously looking at operating electric buses in pedestrian areas. With LCT not wishing to incur the costs of development, the Government department agreed to fund the two prototypes. This suited the manufacturer who could design and develop machines without the need to have guaranteed large-scale further orders. CLE had already been talking with LCT and had carried out route trials and evaluations using a traditional demonstration vehicle. In recognition of the work already done by CLE, they were chosen to build the new buses. CLE purchased two Leyland 900 FG chassis, minus all the normal engine-powered equipment, and electrical conversion took place at Tredegar. The Willowbrook Company, a well-known builder of bus bodywork, constructed the bodies. Designed to seat nine passengers with standing room for a further 17, the buses had a top speed on the level of 25mph. They had a range of around 35 miles per charge. Each vehicle had a 9.5ton gross vehicle weight and was powered by Exide batteries of 110 cells (220V), driving through a 24hp traction motor and controlled by a thrysistor electronic unit. The vehicles were completed during early 1972 and began trials with several bus operators. Between March that year and October 1974 trials took place with 12 operators in 14 towns and cities. However, the trial performance did not convince the operators and both vehicles were returned to the DTI who gave them to a museum. One was subsequently scrapped.

Other Hawker Siddeley group companies made electric vehicles too, including Ormskirk-based Brook Victor Electric Vehicles Ltd who were acquired in 1974. They had originally made the Victor range of BERVs together with a range of industrial trucks. However, when acquired by Brook Motors Ltd, the road vehicles were removed from the range and the truck business was renamed. CE were fortunate as many Brook Victor trucks were of a specialist nature with many one-offs made to customer demands. The new trucks complemented the former Brush products well, and provided an enviable range of machinery available for horizontal movement. Brook Victor products continued manufacture in Ormskirk rather than Tredegar.

Compton Electricars were fortunate to have several good sales agents and Oxford Electrics, based on the outskirts of Oxford, were no exception. Around late 1974 and early 1975, they designed a new type of vehicle for the delivery of dairy products. This featured an entirely new layout.

Britannia Airways chose the E/Fg30 long-wheel based chassis on which to mount mobile stairways used for boarding and disembarking aircraft.

The product consisted of a half-cab for the driver, with a walkway through the centre of the deck and generous storage lockers above the deck for groceries and other food products. By the side of the cab – on the nearside only - was a platform with two steps to floor level. This allowed the operator to collect goods from the centre of the vehicle and walk off at the front. Access was also provided at the rear and milk from crates could be handled from the sides as normal. The storage space was particularly useful when a business sold bread and pre-packed vegetables in addition to dairy products. Oxford Electrics called their new machine Oxcart, not inappropriately. Realising the possibilities for nationwide sales of this machine, they approached CE, asking if they would be interested in manufacturing the vehicle at Tredegar. The request was favourably received. Using the well-proven F chassis as the basis for the new model, and building a body to the same design as the Oxcart, a demonstration example was built and used on trial in the Bristol area. CE called the new model Thruline, with several pre-production examples sold before the

vehicle's official December 1975 launch in Oxford, Birmingham and Manchester. The body was built of metal sections and metal cladding with the exception of the roof which was glass fibre with a translucent central section. On one side of the upper deck the food storage lockers were open, while the other side had up and over lockable doors. One main advantage was that it was no longer necessary to shuffle the milk crates; they could now be accessed from the central walkway or the outside. On October 1, 1976 the last of the acquisitions took place when Oxford Electrics became part of the CE business.

HUNTING FOR SURVIVAL

The declining market for new vehicles in the dairy trade and in other areas such as baking, laundry services and the municipal sector, persuaded the company to target the increasingly lucrative market for mass produced vans,

When this vehicle was photographed the end was not very far away for the Tredegar factory. Sporting the Electricar logo the vehicle was an urban delivery van built on a K-series chassis and part of a large order completed for Initial Laundry Services.

largest linen hire organisation, successfully used these vans and over the years built up a fleet of more than 20 vehicles. Acceleration on the Urban Delivery Vehicle was via an electronic controller, through a heavy duty series-wound traction motor which gave a 25mph top speed on the level. During 1975 CE won good press coverage following the distribution of a press release in October that year. They were able to exploit the success of Initial Services to their own advantage. The release didn't concentrate on the vehicle itself, more on the financial advantages of using one.

During the mid-1970s another new vehicle was introduced, designed to break into the remaining market for milk delivery vehicles. The F90/48/TS was a two-speed electric dairy vehicle. It was developed by Crompton-Electricars to provide a vehicle which could perform as quickly on former diesel or petrol rounds, but with the operating economy of an electric vehicle.

The vehicle was based on the standard F model, with a 4.530kg gross vehicle weight (90cwt) and 1,554kg (30cwt) payload. The range was greatly increased to a maximum 83km (52 miles) with full payload and no stops. The 48-cell 96V battery gave a level top speed of 21mph. A silicon controlled rectifier (SCR) electronic controller was fitted as standard, providing infinitely variable speed control on short start/stop duties to reduce battery energy consumption. In September 1975 a report was published on a trial conducted by the RAC on the two-speed Urban Delivery Van. The controller was important in achieving the two-speed function. The trial report stated: "The two-speed unit consists of an electronic solid-state control module, which is used in conjunction with the SCR controller. When starting from rest the driver depresses the foot switch and the vehicle accelerates. The second speed selection only becomes available to the driver after a pre-selected time and road speed have been attained; by this means it is impossible for the vehicle to achieve more than approximately 14mph for an initial period of 20 seconds, irrespective of driver demands. After this delay, a light and buzzer indicates to the driver that second speed may be selected by pressing a button situated on the dashboard, thereby allowing speeds in excess of 14mph to be achieved."

The report described the five set tests conducted with a dummy load to maximum capacity. The first was a non-stop run from the factory over 60

especially where the daily range was unlikely to exceed 80km (50 miles). In 1974 the new Urban Delivery Vehicle was built and several demonstrators were made available for field evaluation. Using the well-proven F chassis, with a glass fibre body and having cab and body as an integral unit, the result was an attractive, functional product. The generous load space of 9.6cu m (340cu ft) based on a total gross vehicle weight of 4,320kg (4.25 tons) including the battery, provided an annual operating cost saving of between 30 per cent and 50 per cent when compared to a petrol or diesel engined van. Following successful trials, one company was so impressed by the savings and operational benefits that they ordered eight vans in the first year of production. Initial Services Ltd, Britain's miles. This was repeated three times. Test two measured the reduction in battery capacity with the vehicle stopped 150 times during the run. Then followed a gradient test on three levels, followed by a braking test in which the vehicle was driven at full speed and the brake efficiency recorded on a Tapley meter located in the cab. The final test was designed to record the maximum speed over a measured run. All tests were conducted under the constant surveillance of an RAC observer.

In May 1977 CE organised an event to commemorate the Silver Jubilee of Her Majesty Queen Elizabeth II, running a two-speed standard milk delivery vehicle from Buckingham Palace to Blackpool. Arrival in the west coast resort coincided with the annual conference of the National Association of Co-operative Transport Officials. Using an unladen standard two-speed F model, stops were made for recharging at three of the company's service depots – Oxford, Birmingham and Altringham – before a final charge at Blackpool. According to Electric Vehicles magazine, the longest daily mileage was over 80 miles.

In the late 1970s the electric vehicle industry entered a new era of change. CE were now promoting their products to new markets. For example, the London Electric Vehicle Assessment Scheme was launched, administered as a co-operative between the Department for Industry, the Greater London Council and several vehicle manufacturers. Its primary purpose was to obtain independent operational experience covering a wide variety of suitable applications for delivery vehicles in the payload capacity range of 0.5 to two tonnes. Suppliers included Lucas Industries Ltd in association with Vauxhall Motors and 25 of their Bedford CF vans, Chloride Technical Ltd in association with Chrysler UK and National Carriers Ltd with 25 Dodge Karrier vans, and CE in association with Initial Towel Services Ltd with 12 vehicles. Detailed records were compiled, covering performance, suitability and operating costs. A driver attitude survey was conducted by the GLC to record their views on driving the vehicles in the city. The tests were conducted over a period of time and reported in some detail in the June 1979 edition of Electric Vehicles magazine. This was a timely promotional tool for a Wembley Conference Centre exhibition in October 1980. Drive Electric 1980 was well supported by BERV manufacturers and well attended by representatives

Maintenance duties at a large power station awaited this mobile workshop constructed behind a standard cab on an E/Fg chassis.

of operating companies. They must have been impressed by the display of vehicles in a parade outside the venue.

Into the new decade, production at Tredegar continued with the company's full range of electric vehicles. Industrial trucks were still selling well but orders for road vehicles had slowed considerably. The range of BERVs now included the E/fg, still popular but now uprated to give a gross vehicle weight of 70cwt and known as the E70, incorporating a fully floating rear axle as fitted to the larger F/Fg. The latter now boasted capacities up to two tonnes and was available in standard format or as a two-speed variant. The K model Commando chassis, now in a Mk 3 version, was still offered with the rear entry cab facility and the Urban Delivery Van was now mounted on the K3 chassis instead of the F chassis. In early 1982 the model reference was changed. All vehicles now carried the name Electricar and, instead of a metal badge, the name was printed on adhesive-backed transfers. The change was part of a new house style within the Hawker Siddelely Group and avoided confusion with other group companies having 'Crompton' as part of their title.

During the early 1980s the Pope visited Britain and a mass was held at Pontcanna Fields, Cardiff. Two new K model dairy delivery vehicles were loaned for the occasion, straight off the production line and by permission of Leicester Co-operative Society Ltd who had bought them. The vehicles were painted in papal yellow and white with the papal flag flying from the rear canopies. With a specially adapted deck to mount the small chalices (or ciboria) containing wafers of unleavened bread (the consecrated hosts), the vehicles were driven to the altar for the Pope to bless the bread. They were then driven around the field for priests to distribute as part of the communion service attended by thousands of worshippers.

BEGINNING OF THE END

In 1981-82 the company designed the new NP10. It would be the very last new product they would offer. Eight pre-production prototypes were ordered by the Department for Trade and Industry and these were given to potential fleet users on long-term trial. Six carried normal walk-through van bodies, one had a demountable box body and all were painted in the operators' fleet colours. The manufacturer retained one of the vans for field trials. This vehicle was designed from the ground up by engineering staff at Tredegar. Its heavy duty chassis was capable of carrying a large battery, the bodywork and the payload, and was able to withstand the high performance levels of a traffic-compatible vehicle for which it was intended. With a payload of 1.5 tonnes, a laden speed of 30-35 mph and a minimum range of 50 miles, it was hoped that this would meet the requirements of a large section of the commercial market for localised work. It would mean a 20 per cent saving on overall operating costs of internal combustion engined equivalents. Fitted with high energy batteries and an electronic controller incorporating regenerative breaking, the vehicle took its drive from the motor via a propeller shaft to the rear axle where there were twin tyres. The glass fibre body had a capacity of 10 cubic metres and sliding doors were fitted on each side. It was designed from the outset as an electric vehicle and not as a conversion from an internal combustion engined chassis. Trials were going well, but then events at a high level within the organisation dramatically put an end to the programme. During the latter part of 1982, Hawker Siddeley decided to sell the business as a going concern with a price tag of around £3m. A consortium of the company's distributors put in an offer but they couldn't match the asking price. The only other interest was from a small BERV manufacturer based in the Midlands who acquired the business with a reduced offer. The Tredegar factory was not included as that was owned by the Welsh Development Agency which had succeeded the old Board of Trade. In early 1983, the factory closed, with all machinery and work in progress, moved to the Midlands. With the move came the end of this famous British manufacturer.

The last model to be produced by the company, the NP10, plain white van.